LEARN HOW TO

BACK FLIP

IN 31 DAYS

By
Logan Christopher

WARNING & Disclaimer

Trying to do this move without the proper lead up can lead to injury. I can't tell you how many stories I've heard, or even seen, of bad landings, including broken arms and backs. Be careful!

In truth the content found within this book is for educational purposes only and you shouldn't try this without being under the watchful eye of a qualified instructor. If you choose to neglect this warning you do so under your own risk.

All images, unless otherwise noted, are from my private collection. They are reproduced here under the professional practice of fair use for the purposes of historical discussion and scholarly interpretation. All characters and images remain the property of their respective copyright holders.

Table of Contents

Why the Back Flip?

When I was a young boy I watched super heroes and ninjas on TV and movies. I was always awe struck by what they could do. One move that captured my imagination more than most was the back flip. I thought about just how cool it would be to easily pull off that move anywhere and any time. But it was just a wish at that point. I didn't think it was actually possible. I wasn't a gymnast. I wasn't athletic. Hell, I couldn't even do a pushup as I was a weak, scrawny and uncoordinated kid.

Fast forward about 10 years. I had gotten into strength training particularly bodyweight training. As I started to progress in this I knew I wanted to take it to higher levels so I joined an adult gymnastics class. Considering this class was full of ex-gymnasts I was quite out of my league but I was willing to work. It began with the most basic of moves like rolling, cartwheels and roundoffs but with time it became more complex and the skills got harder.

I began working on the backflip. For me it was a long hard road ahead. I couldn't even go backwards on a trampoline for fear of hurting myself so I really had to go piece by piece.

But after a few months of work I had it down. I was effortlessly throwing back flips in class and soon outside. I had mastered a life long dream.

Just practicing the backflip outside at parks I'd frequently have kids, and even adults, exclaim how awesome it was and how they wish they could do it too. Well, now you can.

While you can learned the form of a back flip in many places, its actually quite useless to you. Instead you need to learn the processes for gaining the skill in performing this movement. Sure there are some that can do this easily on their first try, but most people are not there and by trying that you can seriously hurt yourself.

In this book I offer you not just one step-by-step system, the preferred one but one that requires equipment and spotters, and also a second one, that can be done 100% on your own. Lastly, there is a mix of the two for those that can move even faster.

In addition, you'll find tips on the hardest part of the backflip, overcoming the fear that holds you back. This book is short but it teaches you everything you need to master this skill and more.

You'll find the terms back flip and back tuck used interchangeably as they are referring to the same move.

Warmups

When you master the back flip soon enough you'll be able to do it with no warmup at all, any time that you want. However, when you're beginning it is best not attempt this. By following a certain sequence you'll be best setup physically to learn and practice this skill best.

<u>Dynamic Stretching</u>

Do not static stretch. One study has shown how it actually lessens strength and increases the risk of injury if done before training. Instead do some dynamic work. This includes:

- Forward and Backwards Bends
- High Kicking
- Touching Your Toes
- Squats
- Arm Circles

Do a few repetitions of each (10 to 20) and you'll be good to go.

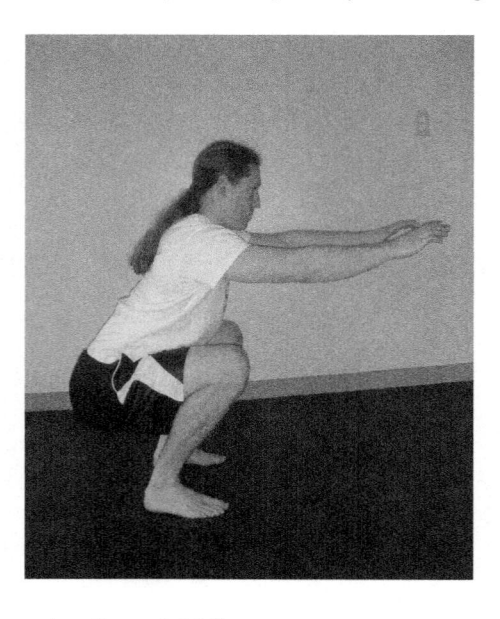

Backwards Roll

The backwards roll, also known as a backwards somersault, done on the ground is useful in teaching the body to travel the same sort of path it will be doing in the back tuck. By teaching this movement pattern here the body can become use to the movement in a no stress environment.

This backwards roll involves going over the neck and head. If you've never done this it can be somewhat uncomfortable. Make sure to practice it on a soft surface. A gymnastic floor works well. If you don't have that then carpet or grass will suffice. You may need to begin with forward rolls to get use to this first.

This is not the same as a parkour or martial arts roll where you'd go over either shoulder.

Practice doing this movement from a position where you're lying on your back with your arms overhead. Then tuck and pull your legs hard to generate the momentum to carry you over. This is exactly the same tuck you'll be doing the back flip. If you can do it without placing your hands on the ground to help you, even better. Practice this 3 to 5 times.

Back Handspring

The back handspring can be a useful lead-up stunt to the back flip. Because you stay closer to the ground and keep your hands overhead the entire time it often feels safer to do. By doing a couple of these you'll work a similar acrobatic ability.

Be warned though. The jump and trajectory are quite different in this move than in the back flip. Thus it can mess you up, rather than help as you may find you stop jumping straight up for the flip after doing this. My advice is to experiment and find if this helps you.

How to do the back handspring will be covered in a later section.

Practice this 2 to 3 times.

<u>Jump High</u>

To warmup a few jumps will suffice. Practice steps 1 through 4 of the back flip form so you'll gain a good take off and trajectory. You can work on jumping higher and straight up as well as the form involved.

Practice this 3 to 5 times.

UNLEASH YOUR INNER ACROBAT

For many more tumbling moves that can help you build up to back flips and increase your acrobatic skills check out Tumbling Illustrated. This step by step guide gives you 248 moves you can master. It's not nearly as complete in detail as this but there are many moves you can get started with right away.

Go to www.LegendaryStrength.com/tumbling-illustrated/

Back Flip Form

Here is a break down of the back flip form. While extremely important, realize that this won't help you without the processes in order to be able to do this. You need to ingrain the skill piece by piece to be able to do it.

These pictures were taken from a video since it was too difficult to get each step just by snapping stills, even in action mode.

Note that there is much room for improvement in my back flip. My jump could be more vertical in these pictures with more extension and my tuck could be much harder. Still that shows you that you don't need to be perfect to pull off this move. Good enough is good enough.

Step 1 - Start with your feet shoulder width apart. When you get good at backflips this can be changed to make them tougher but for now you want to start with this easy position. Start with your arms held up high or at least at chest level. Your head should be held straight with our eyes looking forward.

Step 2 - Bend the legs back, squatting slightly (less than 90 degrees) and bending at the hips as your arms come down to the sides of your legs or back even further. Keep your eyes facing forwards. Breathe in.

Step 3 - Explode and jump straight up with your hands shooting high and exhale hard. Many people think you'll want to jump backwards but you don't. The more height you have here the easier the flip becomes so jump straight up. Do not begin to arch your back. In addition the hands being above your head can offer some protection if the flip doesn't go right. By learning this habit, even if you under perform, it can often be turned into a back handspring instead of a back flip. Continue looking forwards as this helps to jump high and not back. You'll notice that in the photo I'm looking back a bit which starts too much of an arch.

Step 4 - While you don't want to pause during the back flip, you don't start the second phase, the tuck, until you reach the apex of the jump. Too many people are overly concerned with getting the move over with, that they start this process too soon. You must fight this urge and get full extension with your body. Ideally you want to be straight up and down with the ground. In this photo I am going too far back.

Step 5 - Now comes the tuck. Pull hard on your knees as if doing an aggressive knee or leg raise. The tighter the tuck the easier the flip is to pull off. I'll admit, I'm not the best at this part of the equation. I tend to back flip with only a semi tuck position, but since I jump high I can easily pull it off.

Step 6 - As you begin to rotate over your arms will come back to your sides. This natural movement helps in finishing the tuck. Continue to pull your legs around and reach your knees to your chest. I'm beginning to straighten them too early in this portion of the movement.

Step 7 - When you've come close to fully rotating over you'll begin to extend the legs.

Step 8 - Make sure to bend your knees as you touch the ground. For best results you'll want to be landing on your full foot and not just the balls of the feet. The hips will also be bent to cushion you from the shock. You may be bent over when you land and as you get better you can become more upright.

Equipment for Back Flipping

In the next section is the exact process I used to master the back flip. For this one a certain amount of equipment is needed which is listed below.

Trampoline

This is a very useful tool for learning the back flip. Although many people can do a backflip on a trampoline, it doesn't necessarily translate into doing a standing back flip. But this is a useful starting point for many. Make sure you have a full size trampoline and not just a mini rebounder.

THE ULTIMATE GUIDE TO BOUNCING,
FLIPPING AND TWISTING ON A TRAMPOLINE
Use the trampoline to master your acrobatic skill. It's a must for the would be gymnast or parkour athlete. There's no safer way to learn how to control you body and get it to do everything you want it to do. Learn 50 complete trampoline stunts.
Go to www.LegendaryStrength.com/trampoline-handbook/

Crash Pad

A crash pad is usually a 4' by 8' foot pad although they come in different sizes. If you don't have access to this many people effectively use an old mattress and or couch cushions to form the same sort of padding. The biggest aim here is not just safety but also getting you to feel safe.

Folding Gymnastic Mats

As before you don't need the professional version. Anything stable you can jump off of will work. The main thing you want though, is a way to incrementally change the height. This is a key to increasing what you can do in the back tuck bit by bit.

Doing a back flip on a hill can work but is not quite as good. First the angle of you feet will be slightly off. And being on the hill will tend to send you back more rather than jumping straight up. It can work but it is not optimal.

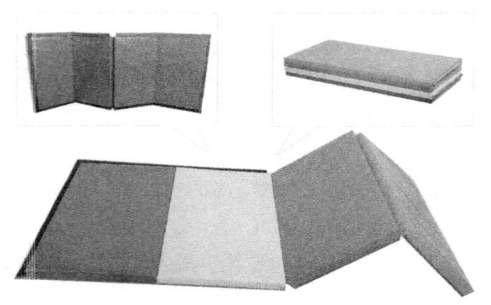

Whatever you do jump off of, make sure it is stable! If there is any chance of it moving when you jump don't use it.

<u>Spotter</u>
How to spot a back flip will be covered in the next section.

A word on using these steps. Just because you've made it to step 7 doesn't mean you never return to step 6 or anything easier. As part of the warmup process you're likely to begin a few steps before where you're at, especially if its been a few days since you're last practice. Go back to a spotter for your first jump for the day if you need to it, then move forward from there. Each time just try to get a little further than before. Even small improvements in form or how easy it feels are an important step.

<u>Pool</u>
The pool can be used in a couple of ways. The first is to learn how to go backwards while submerged. Make sure you plug your nose thought.

Secondly, you can backflip off of the side of the pool into it, assuming its deep enough. This will change up your form as you'll have to jump backwards instead of straight up, but you will not have to worry so much about the landing. You can use this method in conjunction with some of the others to build up to a standing back flip.

Rings

If you have hanging rings at the right height this tool can also be used to learn how to get your body to go over backwards. The proper height would be overhead but no so much you can't touch the ground with your feet.

Grab a hold of the rings. Jump up and flip around. You can use your arms to assist in the movement. When you've come close to fully rotating it is best to let go of the rings and land. What you want to avoid is coming down with momentum and catching with your arms as they'll be in a precarious position.

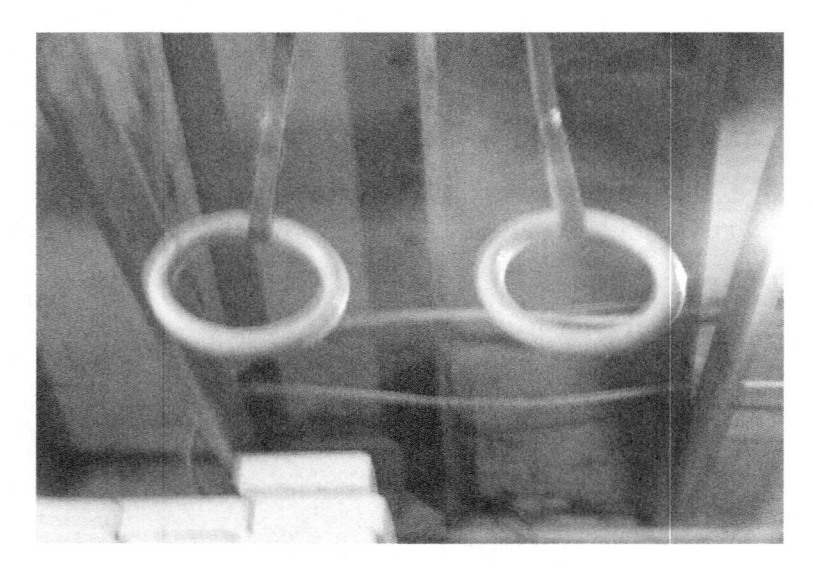

Need a pair of gymnastic rings? Grab the kind I personally use at www.LegendaryStrength.com/go/rings

How I Learned the Back Flip Step by Step

This is the nine step process I used to go from, being to scared to go over backwards on a trampoline to doing backflips outside whereever I wanted. Its a long process but allows the least athletic of people to eventually gain this skill.

Note that while I break it up into nine steps here, there really are even more. You can use additional steps as mentioned if you need them.

Step 1 - Flying Backwards Roll

Like I mentioned before, I couldn't even go backwards on a trampoline. Any attempt to do so and I would immediately turn. Thus I wasn't even safe to spot as I likely could have taken out my instructor. Hence you have this drill.

Here's what it looks like. The raised pad should be about shoulder height. Jump up and backwards with full extension and land on it with your body outstretched. Immediately, go into a backwards somersault. Its kind of like breaking the two pieces down with the pad in the middle to catch you from phase 1 to 2.

This trains your ability to go straight backwards and trust that everything will be okay which is very important in getting over the fear and having your body bail out of a back flip.

Since this requires more equipment than most have you could effectively get the value in it from the Jump High and Roll Backwards drills laid out in the warmup section. There are the two pieces just spread apart.

You can also do a modified version of this with pads on the ground. You won't get the full extension of a jump but instead you jump backwards landing about on your upeer back//shoulder area with the legs pulling up and over you.

Step 2 - Spotted Back Flip on a Trampoline

Once the prior movement felt easy it was time to put it together for real. Using a trampoline you will jump high then tuck. The spotter helps you over and makes sure you land. Since you're on a trampoline you don't have to worry much about generating the force to jump high as you can easily bounce very high. The primary focus will be on tucking.

If you have a wide open trampoline, even if you bail out, its not likely you'll hurt yourself. Make sure you trust your spotter to make sure you get over safely.

Step 3 - Back Flip on a Trampoline

Once you can easily do it with a spotter its time to remove the spotter. The easiest way to do this is to keep the spotter there in the ready position, but only to help you if you need it. Once you get that, you can move get rid of the spotter entirely and practice the move over and over by yourself.

Play around with the movement working to make your tuck easier and better each time.

Step 4 - Spotted Back Flip on a Raised Platform into a Crash Pad

In the beginning you'll want to start on about 18 to 24 inches going into an 8 inch crash pad. At least that's what I did. The purpose of the crash pad it to protect you in case you don't land well.

The purpose of the raised platform is to give you extra room in which to pull off the move. At this point its likely that your jump will be too far back and not high enough (as that happens to almost everyone). Of course, here you'll want to make sure you jump back just slightly. And you'll likely need to improve your tuck even more.

Since you have to string together the jump and tuck for the first time yourself you'll want to bring back the spotter for this step.

Step 5 - Back Flip on a Raised Platform into a Crash Pad

As before, once you have successfully done it with the spotter you can do away with him or her, in the same manner as before.

Work on it until it becomes easy at this step which leads right into the next...

Step 6 - Step by Step Lowering of the Raised Platform

The reason for a height you can incrementally change about an inch at a time is to make a seamless progression. When one height is easy you go down just a little bit and try again. Work at wherever you're at.

This part of the process is likely the longest of all the steps and you'll have to refine your jump and tuck to get better so you can pull it off with less and less space.

Step 7 - Level Back Flip into a Crash Pad

Eventually you'll get to level ground with a same height from the platform to the crash pad. Congratulations! You are almost there.

Step 8 - Back Flip on the Gymnastic Floor

Although you've accomplished a level height, it can be a mental hurdle for each of the next steps, rather than just physical ones. To go from having the safety of the crash pad to a harder floor is a step for some people.

To make this easier you can work into smaller crash pads. There are often 4" and even 1" pads available you can put to use if you need smaller steps here.

Step 9 - Back Flip Outside

Another mental hurdle is then transferring this from the gymnastics facility (if that's where you've been doing it) to outside. Once again, although its all level ground, the safety factor can come up for some people.

A part of this as well if that you can't warmup in the same way. While with the equipment you can warmup with an 8" added height, then 4", then the floor, you may not have that ability to work incrementally outside. I recommend you make the skill super easy in the gym before going outside. Also practice doing it there with limited or no warmups at all.

There are also further steps to go. Doing the back flip on grass is different (mentally at least) than on concrete. We'll talk about taking the flip even further in a later section.

One place like to practice was in sand. The problem with sand is that it will dramatically cut down on your jump. But if you bring something like a sheet of wood to place in the sand and jump off of you can forgo this. Then the sand will offer some protection without having a padded surface.

How to Spot a Backflip

Spotting a backflip is actually quite easy to do. You'll want to have someone who has done this before if its the first time you're going head over heels.

Step 1 - Stand to the side of the person doing the back flip.

Step 2 - Place one hand in the center of the lower back. This hand can even grab onto their shirt. The other hand is placed above the back of the knee joints on the underside of the thighs.

Step 3 - When the person jumps, the hand on the back is used to support while the hand on the legs is used to flip the person over.

Step 4 - The hands should only let go once the person is completely over.

You'll likely feel the one side is better than the other. I personally feel that my dominant right hand should be on the back to support while the left hand is on the legs. Therefore I am standing to the left side of the person.

This same method of spotting works for the back handspring too.

Notice the hands behind the low back and under the thighs

How to Learn the Back Flip Step by Step with No Equipment or Spotters

No everyone has access to a gym with the right equipment. While spotting can easily be learned sometimes that's not even available. Is there a way to learn the backflip without all that? The answer is yes.

Credit goes to the Tapp Brothers for sharing this method to me. You can check out their great Parkour training info at www.LegendaryStrength.com/go/parkour/

While this method is not as safe or incrementally step-by-step as the other one it can work if you need it. If nothing else this will teach you some other skills or methods in training the back flip. You can end up doing some sort of hybrid of the two it you feel that that will work best for you.

Step 1 - Do a Cartwheel

You need to learn how to do a cartwheel to start this process. The cartwheel is easy to do, though most people cannot do a good form one without some practice.

Step 2 - Do a Twisting Back Handspring

The reason for the cartwheel is that you're going to do a back handspring/cartwheel hybrid in this step. Instead of going straight to your side you'll go slightly to the rear. The next time you do a little more, and a little more.

This is not my favorite step. If you start going to your sides it can be hard to get rid of that habit. This I feel like if you can get a spotter and move straight to step 3 you'll be better off.

The end goal is to get to a straight back handspring.

Step 3 - Do a Back Handspring

The back handspring is a great acrobatic movement itself. It involves going backwards like a back flip except that your hands will touch the ground and then you'll come to your feet. It is recommended to use a spotter the first time you do this.

Step a - Start with your feet about shoulder width apart and hands held up high.

Step b - Swing your arms down as you bend your knees and sit back. Your momentum should be backwards as if you're sitting down in a chair. Should you stop the movement at this point you would fall on your butt. You head and eyes are facing forwards.

Step c - Swing your arms up overhead as you jump up and backwards at about 45 degrees. (You can experiment with the exact angle that works best for you, since its different for different people, but this is a good starting point.) The upper arms should be by your ears. Your back should be arched but not to arched.

Step d - Your hands will contact the floor. The hands should be about shoulder width apart and the elbows locked out as this will give you the best spring. A common error is to have the arms bent and too wide. Continuing the momentum of your feet over your head.

Step e - Snap your legs down aggressively with your abdominal muscles and your upper body upwards. You should land in a standing position with your hands above your head or in front of you. The knees will be slightly bent in order to cushion the impact of the floor.

A common mistake is to not get enough spring to bring you to your feet, thus ending in a position on all fours, or with the feet on the ground but the torso bent over instead of upright. This can be caused by the arms not being locked out, spread too wide, and not giving a push with them that helps to send you over. In addition you have to whip or spring around to get to this position.

If you have one available use a spotter the first few times you do this move. Spotting is done in the same manner as the back flip.

Step 4 - Do a Back Flip

In the back handspring you don't leave the ground for very long. Once your feet leave you're quickly on your hands. But here we're going to stretch that time out. Instead of jumping back you'll start jumping higher and higher. This means you'll change when you land on your hands and how far your body is wrapped around by the time that happens.

Eventually as you increase your vertical jump higher, you'll get to a point where you miss your hands. Congratulations you've just done a back flip. Now its just a matter of cleaning it up so that you don't just barely miss your hands but can move them into the regular back flip position (that is overhead then lowered to the legs). The form will change slightly throughout this but that is what is needed for this method.

Fastest Method Possible with Limited Equipment?

For me, I had to go through the 9 steps mentioned earlier. For others you may not need as much. Plus I didn't have this guidebook to tell me what to do. This method only requires a spotter and just some padding.

<u>Step 1 - Work on the high jump and backwards roll. Put it together in the flying backwards roll.</u>

<u>Step 2 - Have a spotter help you to learn the back handspring.</u>

<u>Step 3 - Start doing the back handspring on your own.</u>

<u>Step 4 - Have a spotter help you to learn the back flip.</u>

<u>Step 5 - Start doing the back flip on your own.</u>

For fastest results the back flip, and everything leading up to doing it, can be practiced every day. While it does take some effort to jump high and pull to tuck, unless you're doing tons and tons of reps won't be sore, or unable to practice again the next day.

In each session you may get to a point where your height or pull just wasn't what it was before. Stop there. This is not a move to practice when fatigued. Allow rest time between reps and call it a day when you need to.

If you work on it each day you'll stay focused and be able to make fast progress. The title promises 31 days to a back flip. This may or may not happen for you. It depends on your consistency. Some people may gain it faster. Others will take longer. The thing is if you follow the processes it will work.

Advanced Back Flipping

So you've learned the back flip. What now? Here are a few ideas that will take it further and how to advanced to the next level.

Shoes

Jumping barefoot and jumping with shoes on are a different matter. The shoes may way you down slightly change your jump ever so little, but the harder part may be the tuck. This is not a big advancement in difficulty but it is something. Be sure you're ready for it if you haven't done it before and are about to try.

Repeats

I made it my goal to do ten back flips in a row. As soon as I landed I would ready myself and jump right back again. By doing this you'll get lots of practice in a short period of time. The hard part about this is that you'll get dizzy and your jump is likely to get less vertical as you go on.

There are two versions of this. One is to not re-position your feet after landing and go immediately. The other is to get into your ready position with a step or two and then go. Try both.

<u>Weight</u>

This is not really a recommended one but I have done it. Holding light dumbbells in each hand you do a backflip. This idea came to me from oldtime strongmen such as Sandow who were said to do a back flip over a chair holding 50 lbs.

The most I ever did was 10 lbs. Be forewarned. This dramatically changes this rotation of the back flip. It's also much more dangerous as you have weights in your hand. If you have to bail or don't make it around, it could end badly. Once again, it's not recommended.

A weight vest (making sure it was secured well) could be a different matter, but I haven't tried that one out. Personally, I think there are better ways to train this skill at higher levels.

Backward somersault over a low chair, carrying 50 lbs. in the hands.

Height

If you can do it on level ground, can you do it by jumping up a height? Try with just two inches then four and so on. I've watched someone do a back flip up onto a 16" inch height. Of course, the chances for under rotating increase here and you could jam your feet or worse.

Stance

Try changing your stance. The shoulder width position is the regular stance but this move becomes tougher by changing it up. Try it with your legs closer together up to feet touching.

You can also put one foot in front of the other. By improving this you could eventually do a back flip on a railing. Make sure you practice it just on a line on the ground, many, many times before you do an actual railing though.

Twisting

Add a 180 to the backflip and you've jumped up the coolness factor of this move. Practice your spinning and then add then add it to the back flip exercise.

Layout

Instead of tucking you can do a back layout. This means your body is in an extending position. This is normally reserved for when you have more space, like when jumping off of something.

Combination

The backflip can be combined in many ways with many different exercises. For one it can be done in combinations with roundoffs or other acrobatic moves.

It could also be combined with strength training. I remember seeing a recent circuit that involved a 200+ lb. snatch, back flips and full range handstand pushups. A great combination if you ask me.

Overcoming Fear

If you haven't noticed the way this entire process of achieving the back flip is setup to overcome your fear step by step. I don't know if anyone was more scared of doing this move in the beginning than I was. I don't know if anyone had less body awareness to get my body to do what was needed in the beginning. But by following this process I was able to gain this skill for good.

A big part of overcoming your fear is to feel safe. By having the proper equipment around you in the form of pads that will protect you if you fall you're freed up to focus on the skill at hand. A competent spotter will do just the same. Like I mentioned going from having a spotter to the spotter being right there, in case they're needed, can be an important step.

So can the steps from level ground onto a mat to level ground without a mat. When you make it more step by step you can bridge the safety you feel in one level of progression to the next. A big jump in progressions will often not bridge this feeling of safety. Use as much of this, or as little as needed.

Whatever you can do to feel more safe is good, because you actually will be more safe in not improperly doing the move. Most of the danger comes in not fully committing to it, but in trying to bail out at the top. In trying to protect yourself, you mind, could actually be what causes the danger.

All that is good, but there is one more drill you can do that can instantly erase fear.

Peak Performance Blowout

I learned this drill from John La Tourrette, Ph.D. in Sports Psychology. It is one form of Energy Psychology that only takes a few seconds to do. I'll get to how to do it in a second but first let's show what it can do for you. In fact, I used it successfully today.

At a seminar I was attending I mentioned that I could do a back flip. I was put on the spot and asked to show it. Since we were in a low ceiling building we had to go outside. Here's the thing. It had been at least 5 months since the last time I had done a backflip. I just hadn't practiced it in quite some time. And I know from previous experience that the fear tends to come back even though I know the skill well, as does my body.

I walked over to a grassy area that was nearby. This was preferable to the concrete for me. Then I did this simple drill. Within seconds I was confident in my ability again. I did the back flip. Everyone clapped, hooted and hollered.

It can make that big of a change. This isn't the only time I've used it and it won't be the last. I've also taught it to many others who have successfully used it to overcome challenges and instill confidence in themselves.

What you do rub the area where your torso meets your arm with your fingertips. (If your arm was chopped off, this is where they would sow it back on.)

As you do this you say out loud, "Even though I'm scared shitless of doing this backflip, I deeply love and accept myself."

This statement can be modified to fit you better but its what I personally use and it works for me.

Without taking the time to go into how and why this works (that would take a whole book this size) I encourage you to just try it for yourself and see. If you want to learn more about it check out *www.ThinkAndGrowStrong.com*

Extra Resources

Want more strength and bodyweight skill? Check out all of the below.

The Ultimate Guide to Handstand Pushups
Get stronger and learn how to do this King of bodyweight exercises. Build up to your first rep than move onto freestanding and full range versions. This is the most complete instruction you'll find on this subject anywhere.
www.LegendaryStrength.com/ultimate-guide-to-handstand-pushups/

Secrets of the Handstand
The Only Handstand Getting System Available Today. Get step-by-step instructions to learn how to master a 30 second freestanding handstand in as short a time as possible. Guaranteed!
www.HandstandMastery.com/

Front and Back Lever Training
Learn how to master the front and back lever in 6 simple steps. You'll also find out about dynamic exercises, changing grips and more.
www.LegendaryStrength.com/front-and-back-lever-training/

Also be sure to grab my **five free special reports** only available
www.LegendaryStrength.com

- The Strongman Manifesto
- Peak Performance Trinity
- How to Get Started with the Handstand
- Get Grounded
- 10 Biggest Mistakes in Mental Training for Strength & Athletics

Printed in Great Britain
by Amazon

33935499R00030